SATIS
A SCIENTIST'S GUIDE

SUPER TECHNICOLOUR EDITION

LEO LAFFERTY-WHYTE, Ph.D

TABLE OF CONTENTS

DEDICATION

This book is dedicated to all us folks who may not be leaping out of bed with joy every morning but are determined to make today better than yesterday.

Keep moving forward.

Thank you for purchasing the

SUPER TECHNICOLOUR EDITION

of

Life Satisfaction: A Scientist's Guide!

To find out more about exclusive offers available to you as a thank you please go to:

WWW.TRIPLEHCOACHING.COM/STE.HTML

THE TRIPLE 'H' PRINCIPLE

IN THIS SECTION YOU WILL LEARN

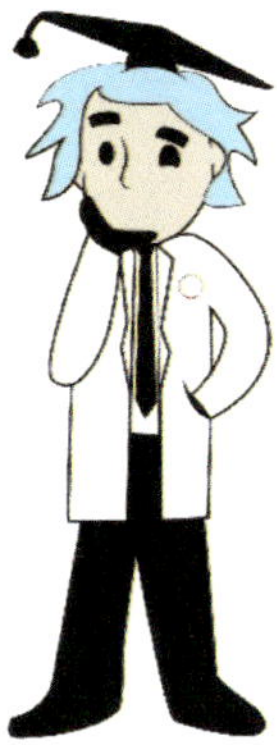

- **WHY BEING 100% HAPPY 100% OF THE TIME IS UNREASONABLE**
- **WHAT THE TRIPLE 'H' PRINCIPLE IS**
- **WHAT EACH OF THE 'H' PRINCIPLES REPRESENTS**
- **THE CONCEPT OF LIFE CURRENCY**
- **WHY IS THIS BOOK ISN'T FOR YOU (MAYBE)**

Personal satisfaction is the most important ingredient of success.

Denis Waitley

People have this strange idea that life coaches spend their days bouncing around the world in a state of perpetual bliss. After all, if we have all these tools at our fingertips for maximizing life satisfaction we must feel great, right?

I hate to burst the bubble. Life coaches suffer from the same terminal disease as you – humanity. We fall, binge, make poor decisions, procrastinate and lose our way just like the rest of you.

No one has it completely worked out. Even the Dalai Lama is on a constant journey of self-improvement. In fact, I strongly recommend that you quickly run in the opposite direction of any life coach or person that tells you otherwise.

Why aren't we bouncing around like care-free bunnies in a green field?

Doesn't that prove that life coaching doesn't work?

Actually, quite the opposite in my opinion. As human beings what makes us happy changes on a daily/hourly basis. The ability therefore to be 100% happy at 100% of the time is somewhat of an unreasonable expectation.

What *is* achievable though is maximizing our potential satisfaction at that current moment. Prioritizing what we need to work on and maximizing our potential.

Life is not static and so we should always be adapting, improving and growing – that's where a life coach or mentor is crucial. They provide a system to identify and action what you need to work on as well as crucial guidance, support and accountability on that journey.

SHARING THE VIP KNOWLEDGE

Not everyone is in the fortunate position to be able to afford a life coach though. Not everyone is ready for that level of commitment. Not everyone likes the idea of having someone else involved in the private parts of their lives. I get it.

In this book I'm therefore going to share with you my secret sauce. The method that I use many times to help my VIP clients, as well as myself, to achieve their dreams and maximize their overall satisfaction.

This method has evolved over the past 20 years, throughout which I've been using it on myself. It changes (and continues to change) as I've incorporated various techniques and exercises inspired by scientific evidence on human psychology, motivation and persuasion as well as my own experience working with different types of individuals.

I call it the Triple 'H' Principle.

In brief, the concept is that there are three main areas of our lives that affect our overall level of satisfaction. When one (or more areas) are particularly low or out of balance – we feel unsatisfied, unhappy and frustrated.

The three 'H's are:

HEALTHY

These are the fundamental areas of our lives that we need to be at maximum in our day-to-day lives to stand any chance of feeling content.

Think of Healthy as the basics, the foundations or the bedrock of a house.

Typical topics for Healthy include physical and mental health but also areas like financial health and relationships.

HAPPY

These are the larger and longer-term areas that may not be day-to-day but still have a large impact on our overall levels of satisfaction and joy.

Not things you can necessarily change in a day but they do have a big impact on your daily mood.

Think of Happy as those things that build on top of the foundations. The walls, the roof and the doors and windows of your satisfaction house.

Typical topics for Happy include career satisfaction, ambitions, achievements and appearance.

HARMONIOUS

These are the big things, the topics that are bigger than us as a person but matter. They are also about balance. Keeping your life in balance and your overall sense of peace.

Think of Harmonious as the location of your satisfaction house. For some people that's a gorgeous cul-de-sac. For others it is a cottage in a woodland. Some people want a high rise flat in a busy city.

Typical topics for Harmonious topics include work:life balance, legacy, level of routine in your life and self-esteem.

Now you might not agree with which of the three principles a particular topic has been placed in. You also might not agree with the names of the three principles themselves.

In reality though, the actual name of the category that a topic is in doesn't matter. It is the groupings that are important. It is the concept of layers of factors that contribute to your overall contentment that all need attention.

As you will see later, dividing them up this way allows us to ensure that we're tackling all of the contributing factors and not just focusing all your efforts at one level.

It is important to note that what is maximum satisfaction for one person may not be the same for all.

Not everyone wants to be a body builder or CEO. The aim of the Triple 'H' principle is to maximize each topic for **your truth.**

LIFE CURRENCY

There are many different ways that people have explained the concept of effort vs satisfaction over the years. In the Triple H Principle we use the concept of Life Currency.

Imagine that your maximal level of satisfaction is represented by a pile of coins. You always have exactly the right number of coins to feel completely and utterly satisfied with your life in your pocket.

To gain full satisfaction you spend these coins on different factors in your life.

The more important something is to you the more Life Coins it will take for you to feel fully satisfied.

Conversely the less important the area the less Life Coins you need to spend to feel fully satisfied with that part of your life.

If you haven't spent all your coins you won't feel fully satisfied.

You spend your Life Coins by putting effort into that area. For example, with fitness you would do some exercise, with education you'd study or with relationships you'd put in the time with the people concerned.

We'll be working out where you're all spent up and where you need to spend more Life Coins as part of the Triple H Process.

WHY THIS BOOK ISN'T FOR YOU (MAYBE)

I'll say upfront that this method might not be for everyone. Why?

- It is quite list oriented so if you hate lists then it's probably not for you.
- It also suits people who like (or need) a bit of structure, struggle to stay organised and need a shove to get/stay motivated. Again if you hate being told what to do (even by yourself) then this method probably won't be for you.
- There's a little bit of mathematics involved at the beginning. Not exactly advanced calculus but if you can't stand maths then this might not be for you.

A BOOK OF TWO HALVES.

In the first section I'll share with you the theory of the Triple H Principles. I'll also give you all of the forms that allow you to apply the Triple H Principles and take control of your life.

I don't believe in asking anyone to do anything I wouldn't do myself. In the second section of this book you will find my month one journey on a cycle of satisfaction improvement. This can be used as a simply as an entertaining story or of course as an example application of the process. Maybe you'll even find some inspiration in the journey.

I think it is also important to say that no book, mentor or coach can magically give you all the answers. They can guide you.

They can give you the tools to help you think about things in a way that you will likely come across them but ultimately the work has to come from you.

I hope that this combination of theory, explanation and example help you to be successful in improving your own life satisfaction.

I'll leave you with one of my favourite sayings – "You haven't failed until you've stopped trying."

Good luck!

WHERE AM I?

IN THIS SECTION YOU WILL LEARN

- WHY YOU'RE NOT HAPPY
- WHAT IS REALLY IMPORTANT TO YOU
- HOW SATISFIED YOU REALLY ARE
- YOUR PRIORITIES
- HOW IT ALL COMES TOGETHER
- HOW IN BALANCE YOU ARE (OR AREN'T)

We're not lost. We're locationally challenged.

John M. Ford

Before you start your journey you need to know where you're starting from. Sounds obvious right? Why then do so many self help and transformation guides miss this step completely?

WHY YOU'RE NOT HAPPY

Many self-help books immediately start instructing you on how to change your life. They take no time to first make sure you really understand how you need it to change to be satisfied in the first place.

They just assume that you have this knowledge...you know what they say about people who assume right? It makes an ASS out of U and ME....

Why is this important though? We think we know what we want; we think we know what it is that would make us happy, right?

If I drop this 30 lbs I'll be happy.

If I can just get a promotion I'll be happy.

If I can just get a boyfriend I'll be happy.

Sound familiar?

You enthusiastically go off pursuing your goal. If you do reach it you suddenly are hit with a devastating realization that you're still not happy. Then what? You choose a new "If I...I'll be happy" and start again. How's that working out for you?

Why are you still not satisfied? In my opinion it is because you're often chasing improvements in areas of your life where you have very few Life Coins left to gain and therefore very little real change in satisfaction will be felt. That isn't your fault though. We are constantly encouraged to chase what society says you should be chasing, i.e. to spend Life Coins only on the things that society can see and ultimately deems important.

In the end, we are all looking for societal approval and instant gratification. However, you're often focusing it all on a single tiny part of your life that has very few Life Coins left to spend (I.e. will make very little difference to your overall sense of satisfaction.) The universe is rarely so simple. In reality, changing just one single thing to fit the societal norm is unlikely to make you feel fulfilled. Human beings are complex organisms after all.

In simple terms you can't work out how to get somewhere without knowing exactly where you are to begin with!

Gaining maximum satisfaction from life therefore is not about a single goal but about getting the right balance. It is about making progress in all the areas that will bring you the biggest payoff. It's about spending those Life Coins in the areas that will bring you most gain!

In reality, I find that it's a case of simple "life mathematics" to balance the three key principles of Healthy, Happy and Harmonious. Calculate what your Life Coin deficit is in each area. Furthermore, each of the three principles needs to be worked on to improve overall satisfaction and they all need to be high scoring to feel that satisfaction.

The first step on the journey to a better life therefore isn't to decide on one thing to chase but instead to work out where you are. Then you can see clearly what you *really* need to work on to bring you the biggest payoff for your effort.

Maximum pay out for minimal effort, sounds good right?

WHAT IS *REALLY* IMPORTANT TO YOU?

So how do we do we work out where we are? Fear not! In the next few pages you will find everything you need and I will walk you through the 8 simple steps to calculating where your Life Coin deficit is, in short, your "life mathematics".

Step 1:

On the next few pages you will find a list of topics divided into the Triple H Principles (Healthy, Happy & Harmonious if you haven't guess yet!).

Select five from each group (so five healthy, five Happy & five Harmonious) that resonate with you.

Some will resonate more strongly than others and some will be very hard to choose between. Some people want all of them on the list, others struggle to identify ones that call strongly too them.

Don’t rush. Take all the time you need on this step.

This will be built upon so take the time to get it right.

HEALTHY

- Personal Development
- Relationships (Friends)
- Relationships (Romance)
- Relationships (Sex)
- Relationships (Family)
- Relationships (Children)
- Relationships (Pets)
- Physical Health
- Independence
- Fitness
- Emotional & Mental Health
- Sleep Quality
- Addictions
- Nutrition

HAPPY

- Career Satisfaction
- Parenting/Carer Skills/Situation
- Career Progress
- Qualifications & Skills
- Ambitions & Achievements
- Financial Situation
- Stress Levels
- Guilt Levels
- Fear Levels
- Hobbies/"Me"/Fun time
- Appearance

HARMONIOUS

- Home life situation/environment
- Work-Life balance
- Self-confidence
- Self-Esteem
- Gender Expression
- Sexuality
- Attitude
- Spirituality
- Adventure
- Legacy
- Helping Others
- Level of Routine in your life
- Appreciation
- Living in the present
- Level of Self-understanding

Step 2:

Enter these into the appropriate rows of the Situation assessment form.

With me so far? Easy right?

HOW SATISFIED ARE YOU REALLY?

Step 3:

For each row under each principle section score how **satisfied** you are with that area out of ten and enter it into the "Current Satisfaction" column (10 being completely satisfied).

Note this is how **satisfied you are NOT how good you think you are at it.** You don't need to be an athlete to be satisfied with you fitness. You just have to be content with the level that it is at. Truly content though – no pretending!

For example, maybe you think you should score a ten in relationships (Romantic) as you have a partner who is always showering you with romantic gestures.

When you ask your gut though it says three. Why?

- Maybe the gestures are too public and embarrass you?
- Maybe they're generic and not personal enough?
- Maybe they are not frequent enough for you really?

So, although by society's standards you may think you should be a ten, you're really not satisfied at all, you're a three. **Put a three in the box**.

For the process to work you need to be **honest & complete**. Don't go filling in what you *think* it should be for each row.

Instead ask your gut how it would score this.

Go with the first number that pops into your head. Aim to put a number in each box within 3 seconds of looking at it. These gut answers are usually the honest ones. (Whether you realize it or not!)

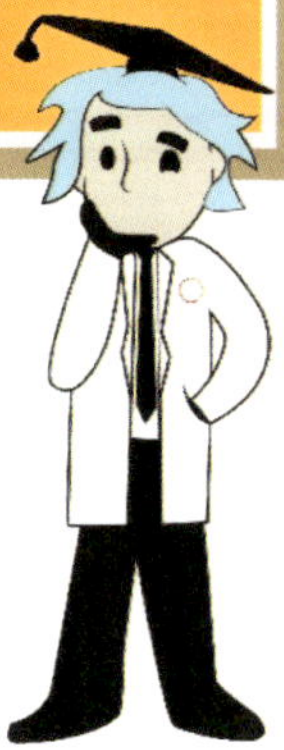

No compromising.

No meeting in the middle.

Put the numbers in the box that are **your truth**.

Sometimes those gut numbers will really surprise you! When you look at them though you'll know whether they are really right or not. That can also sometimes be a painful thing to realise so give yourself some time to come to terms with it before moving on.

Don't rush. If particular rows are niggling at you feel free to do it once, put it down and come back to it and ask your gut again later.

I'll make no pretence that this is always quick or painless. As you'll read in my story I found it neither. In fact, it took me several days just to get the guts to do the check in the first place!

When you actually take the quiet time to work through the exercise you will find it time well spent.

Once you have scored all the areas out of ten it's time get serious.

GETTING YOUR PRIORITIES STRAIGHT

How important are these different things to you? What's their priority in your life?

Step 4:

Rank each row in each principle section in order of their priority to you (where 5 is most important and 1 is least).

Note: **You can only use each number once in each principle section though** (I.e. you can only have one H top priority with a score of 5 and one bottom with a score of 1 in each of the three sections).

Is Career Progress *really* more important to you that Career Satisfaction?

Again, this is not easy but a crucial step to understanding yourself better. Getting this right will ensure that you work on the things that will improve your overall life satisfaction rather than the things you *think* will improve it.

CALCULATING WHERE YOU'VE SPENT YOUR LIFE COINS

Step 5:

For each row multiply the satisfaction score by priority to give your "Spent Life Coins"

"What on earth are spent Life Coins?" I hear you ask!

Spent Life coins are the amount of your total Life Currency (your total pool of life satisfaction) that you have spent on this area. Important things require more coins to feel fully satisfied as they will have a much bigger impact on your overall sense of satisfaction.

The tricky bit is remembering that each row will have a different potential maximum score. So a 7 in a row with a 5 priority is not as impactful as one with a 1 priority. This is often hard to comprehend so. Don't worry the next step will make it easier though.

CALCULATING YOU LIFE COIN DEFICIT

Step 6:

Convert the Spent coins to how many remain to be spent (i.e. deficit) in each category by:

Multiplying the Priority for that row by 10 and then subtracting the Spent Coins.

Take a look at the deficits.

First thing to say is: DON'T PANIC!

It's very common that the results surprise people. Seeing in black and white a quantitative value for where they are lacking in life satisfaction can sometimes be a bit of a shock.

Take a deep breath and remember this is just the start of your journey. After all, if everything was scoring a 10 out of 10 in current satisfaction you probably wouldn't have picked up this book, right? Don't worry we'll come on to improving those scores shortly.

Alternatively, are your scores all very high across the board?

If so can you put your hand on your heart and say you've been 100% honest?

Have you chosen the categories that definitely have the biggest impact on you?

If you can honestly say yes to those two questions, then I congratulate you and ask you to let me know your secret! Maybe you're in that last push to spend those last few coins to make you feel tippy top?

If you can honestly say that you're very satisfied with all the areas of your life then I want you to ask yourself this question before deciding whether to continue with this book:

"If I am so highly satisfied with my life why did I pick up this book in the first place?"

Once you have your answer you'll know what to do.

Step 7:

For each of the Triple H Principles calculate the total the percentage of satisfaction by:

Adding up all the Spent Coins in each principle. Divide the answer by 150. Multiply that answer by 100.

Worry not. If this all sounds a bit much mathematics, then I have an excel sheet that will do it all for you!

It's all available upon request, just drop me an email (info@triplehcoaching.com).

You'll now have overall percentage satisfactions for each of the key principles of your life: Happy, Healthy and Harmonious as well as Life Coin Deficits for various topics within these areas.

Just one more step and all the mathematics is done (I promise!).

Step 8:

Calculate your overall life satisfaction score by adding the three principle overall percentages together and dividing by three.

That's it! All the mathematics is out of the way! Never again will I ask you to multiply or divide. Hurrah!

You now have 4 numbers that will start your journey!

My Healthy % is __________%

My Happy % is __________%

My Harmonious % is __________%

My overall life satisfaction % is ________%

HOW BALANCED ARE YOU?

Take a look at your overall satisfaction percentage.

- Is it what you expected?
  - Higher?
  - Lower?

Take a look at your three Triple H Principle section percentages:

- How in balance are they?
- Are you very Healthy but not very Harmonious for example?

In my experience, without a high score in all three sections no matter how hard you try you won't feel the satisfaction you want in life. This is how billionaires, models and gurus can all still be incredibly unhappy despite a high level of satisfaction in one area.

Everyone's scores will be different! These scores and priorities are yours and yours alone.

There is no right or wrong.

They are not comparable to other people's scores. What you consider an 8 may be what I think of as a 3, for example.

One of the things people often struggle with in this section is priorities.

There are no right or wrong answers when it comes to how we feel.

There is also no judgment for putting your kids below your career. No need to score family highly just because you think it should be. You will only get maximum life satisfaction if you are living your truth, living life according to your priorities.

Now, to be clear, in no way am I saying you should neglect your children for the sake of your career! However, if your career is truly higher on your priorities list for life satisfaction then you will need to look at how to balance those two.

For example, could you take on a Nanny to ensure that the kids get everything they need and that you maximize the quality of the time you do spend with them whilst still getting to focus on your career? That way they will get the benefit of a happy satisfied parent as well as good quality family time. Balance, see?

A WORD OF CAUTION

You may choose to share the results of the exercise with those you care about so they gain a better understanding of where you are at and get their perspective.

However, if you think this will influence how you score things I would **strongly** caution against it.

Ultimately, this is *your* journey and these are your truths. Only aligning with those truths and getting the balance right for you personally will allow you to feel satisfied fully.

People mean well but will also subconsciously trying to do the same in their lives! Their priorities might not align completely with yours and hence it can pull you in a direction that doesn't make you happy. Sound familiar?

Now that you have an idea how balanced you are in terms of the Triple 'H' Principles, your priorities and satisfaction scores we can start to think about how best to move forward and improve both the balance between sections and the scores for each section.

Lastly, I applaud you! You have invested the time to get to know yourself better. That's the best investment you can ever make.

Now the really exciting stuff starts! Now, we need to decide where you want to go and the route to get there!

LIFE MATHEMATICS SUMMARY

1. Enter 5 areas of life from the above lists into each Principle section.

2. Score each area out of 10 for how satisfied you currently feel about it (10 highest score, 1 lowest score)

3. Put each section in order of priority using each number only once (5 highest priority, 1 lowest priority)

4. Multiply Current Satisfaction by Priority to get your Spent Life Coins

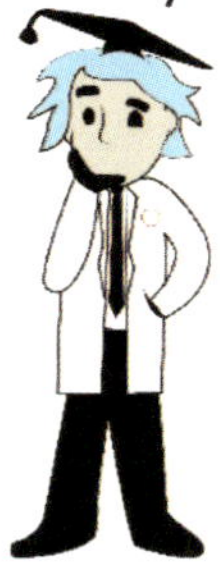

5. Calculate Life Coin Deficits:

   (Priority*10) – Spent Life Coins)

6. Calculate each section's score:

((Total of Section Spent Coins)/150) x 100

7. Calculate overall satisfaction by adding answers from 6 and dividing by 3.

Topic	Satisfaction (1-10)	Priority (1-5)	Spent Life Coins	Life Coin Deficit

HAPPY SECTION % = %

Topic	Satisfaction (1-10)	Priority (1-5)	Spent Life Coins	Life Coin Deficit

HARMONIOUS SECTION % = %

Topic	Satisfaction (1-10)	Priority (1-5)	Spent Life Coins	Life Coin Deficit

WHERE AM I GOING?

IN THIS SECTION YOU WILL LEARN

- HOW TO (AND NOT TO) CHOOSE WHAT TO SPEND LIFE COINS ON
- THE IMPORTANCE OF WHY
- WHAT ACTIONS YOU'RE GOING TO TAKE TO SPEND YOUR LIFE COINS
- WHY YOUR EMPLOYER WAS SMART

I am an idealist. I don't know where I'm going but I'm on my way.

Carl Sandburg

After completing the situation assessment you now know where you are currently at.

Great, I now have a sheet of numbers and what looks like yet another bill to pay! What on earth do I do with that? How does that help me improve my life satisfaction?

That's the reaction I usually get. I get it. It's a lot of work just to find out where you are satisfied and are not. It's worth it though as all our next steps are built on top of this foundation.

We now need to decide what we want to work on. I recommend working in 3-month cycles for this process. In my experience three months is enough time to make significant progress on anything you decide to work on but not such a distant time frame that you will relax into not doing anything.

With that in mind first **we're going to choose one row of each section to build a goal around** to actively improve over the next three months.

As I mentioned previously none of these things exist in isolation though so it's likely that a change in one will impact other rows. There are therefore a few different ways you can choose which topic to work on.

There's no right or wrong method so long as it feels right to you.

Here are a few methods I've used in the past that work well.

BEGINNERS: THE QUICK AND EASY METHOD.

This is a great place to start for your first cycle, if you're unsure what you want to work on or if you're looking to get going quickly without further preparation.

Simply select the row in each principle with the highest Life Coin Deficit.

This ensures that even a small improvement in the score for those rows over the next three months will have a strong impact on how you feel day to day.

RECOMMENDED: THE MAXIMUM BANG FOR MY BUCK METHOD.

This method takes a little more work and time to prepare but will give you the maximum improvement in satisfaction overall and is the method I personally use and recommend.

Take a look at the larger list holistically. How do these different topics in different sections relate to each other?

> Try and draw out a simple spider/tree diagram to show how each row relates to each other. (Take a look at my example sheet in my story for inspiration).

This diagram **will** be a mess. Don't worry about it!

For example, if you spend coins on your Appearance deficit then that will naturally mean that your Nutrition, Fitness and Self-Confidence deficits also decrease (if they aren't already all spent up!) since you'll likely be putting effort into those things to increase that score as well as looking at things like clothes, hair, etc.

The relationships aren't always reciprocal though. In Using the example above, spending Life Coins on your appearance will also likely decrease your self-confidence deficit. However, spending Life Coins on your Self-Confidence deficit alone, through for example positive self-talk, is unlikely to affect your appearance deficit significantly.

I recommend using a different colour for rows from each principle or putting them inside a different shaped box. You can do this on paper, on a mind mapping software tool or on a white board. This will make it easier to ensure you know where they came for selecting step in a moment.

Once you have a rough diagram in place look for the central "hubs" (the ones with the most lines coming out of them). Increasing spending Life Coins in these areas are likely to affect the deficit for more other rows too and naturally increase your general satisfaction by a greater amount.

Select one from each principle that has the most knock-on effects for your overall life.

(Technically it is possible to do this selection process mathematically via various scientific algorithms called network statistics. If you're so inclined feel free but it's not compulsory.)

NOT RECOMMENDED: THE GUT METHOD

Sometimes we have an instinct on what we need to work on regardless of priority and score. If you feel strongly about one particular thing in one principle you're likely to have more coins to spend in that area than you've been honest about.

If it's bothering you that much then it will affect your overall ability to stick to your goals if you don't work on it.

You can select it if you really do feel strongly. I personally don't recommend this method since this often means that people select the easiest ones to work on and often they don't have a big impact on satisfaction overall. You are then left with a disappointed feeling that you put in all that work but the world hasn't changed for you.

Sometimes it is appropriate though to go with your gut feelings. I'd recommend only using this in combination with one of the other methods above to **select no more than one row to work on** (with the other two coming from a more systematic method).

Whatever method you use with your three areas selected, you can enter them below:

In the next 3 months I will focus on spending life coins on:

Healthy: ______________________

Healthy: ______________________

Harmonious: ______________________

THE IMPORTANCE OF WHY

For each selected topic you now need to answer two important questions to start setting yourself up for success:

1. Why will improving this improve my life satisfaction?

HEALTHY

____

____

____

____

HAPPY

____

____

____

____

HARMONIOUS

2. What would life with a 10/10 score for this attribute look like?

HEALTHY

HAPPY

Take your time and answer each of these as fully as possible. The more detail you describe the better. Why are we bothering with this rather than just getting on with taking action?

Interestingly scientific studies have shown that the brain struggles to tell the difference between something that you visualize and something that is really happening!

This effect is something that has mostly been tested in the field of sport where a positive effect on performance has been seen to those athletes who use visualisation techniques ahead of training and events (1) (2).

Therefore, the more detail you can visualize now the more real it will feel, the more you will realise you can do this and the more likely you are to keep striving towards it. By setting up a framework of positivity around that visualization it has also been shown that you can influence your own decision making process and reduce resistance to “sub-optimal” routes (3).

TAKING ACTION TO SPEND LIFE COINS & WHY YOUR EMPLOYER WAS SMART

With those questions answered, mind rewired to the end goal it's time to decide *what* you're going to do to improve it.

Many of you will have used S.M.A.R.T. goals in the workplace for setting annual goals and targets. Many of you will be rolling your eyes at the mention of them I'm sure!

The reason that workplaces use the S.M.A.R.T system is that it works! So, roll your eyes all you like I'd strongly recommend you make your goals:

Specific – Nothing vague. What exactly are you going to do.

Measurable – what can you measure along the way to track progress and success?

Achievable – We're working in a 3-month cycle here so what can you do in that time frame. Be realistic but also don't undersell yourself.

Results-focused – Your goal should be focused on the end-point not the activities you're going to do to get there.

Time-Bound – What date are you going to have achieved this by? In our case we've taken care of this already since it is in the next 3 months. A freebie for you!

	Good Example	Poor Example
Specific	I'm going improve my life	I'm going to improve my life by increasing my Spanish language skills
Measurable	I'm going to learn a language	I'm going to learn 10 Spanish phrases
Achievable	I'm going to be fluent in Spanish	I'm going to learn 10 Spanish phrases first and then learn more
Results-Focused	I'm going to be fluent in Spanish	I'm going to learn 10 Spanish phrases that will help me when travelling.
Time-bound	I'm going to be fluent in Spanish	I'm going to learn 10 Spanish phrases that will help me when travelling in the 3 months.

Example of Good and Poor example of each step of building S.M.A.R.T. goals

A word of caution. Don't try to run before you can walk – it will only lead to frustration and ultimately even less life satisfaction.

Most processes tell you only to work on one goal at a time. Personally, I think this is why we fail to feel fully satisfied after all our hard work. Therefore, I'm asking you **to work on three things concurrently**.

Working on three things does however mean that you need to scale back slightly what those three goals are.

You don't want three massive goals that are time intensive and are going to burn you out in week one! Usually, one large goal with two smaller ones are more easily managed though.

For example, don't aim to learn to be fluent in a new language (*Personal Development*), run a marathon (*Fitness/Ambitions & Achievements*) and setting up a new charity (*Helping others/ Legacy*) **at the same time**.

Choose one as your major goal and scale back the others. If you chose the marathon, for example, then I'd suggest instead learning a set number of phrases in the new language and volunteering for a local charity a few hours a week instead. After this 3-month cycle you might then go back and scale up one of your previous goals to your original ambition whilst scaling down others.

Are you new to goal setting? A long way from your final goal? Time poor? Then there might also be a good reason for only doing one goal at a time in that case.

This is your journey – you set the rules. If you're happy to take a little longer and do one goal at a time then rock on!

You can complete your Goals on the next page. Once complete I'd recommend putting this sheet up, alongside a note of your Why & 10/10 answers, somewhere you'll see it often (the fridge door for example). It will help you stay motivated when times get tough.

HEALTHY: IN THE NEXT 3 MONTHS I AM:

HAPPY: IN THE NEXT 3 MONTHS I AM:

HARMONIOUS: IN THE NEXT 3 MONTHS I AM:

HOW DO I GET THERE?

IN THIS SECTION YOU WILL LEARN

- HOW TO (AND NOT TO) CHOOSE WHAT TO SPEND LIFE COINS ON
- THE IMPORTANCE OF WHY
- WHAT ACTIONS YOU'RE GOING TO TAKE TO SPEND YOUR LIFE COINS
- HOW YOU'RE GOING TO KEEP YOURSELF MOTIVATED
- HOW TO PLAN OUT YOUR FIRST MONTH'S JOURNEY

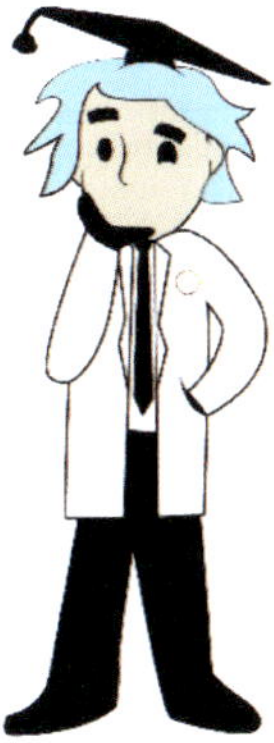

Our goals can only be reached through a vehicle of a plan, in which we must fervently believe, and upon which we must vigorously act. There is no other route to success

Pablo Picasso

We know where we're heading now and what specifically we need to work on.

There's several other exercises about values and your perfect day you could work through one-to-one with a Coach to make it even more powerful but as a basic starting point this is great.

The next step is to work out how we're going to get to our goal endpoint. To avoid overwhelm, we are going to take this month by month, week by week and even day by day.

As the old saying goes don't try and eat the elephant in one bite. Break it down into manageable chunks.

THE POWER OF PAIN AND PLEASURE

Human beings are motivated by two main factors just like any other animal – pain and pleasure.

As intelligent beings we like to think we have evolved past these basic instincts but in reality we are still animals by nature. We still have fight or flight reactions (not always appropriately), we still all have primal urges for sex, community and status (4) .

What's really interesting though, is how pain and pleasure interact and how differently we react to them respectively (5) (6).This is down to various balances of brain chemicals (such as serotonin and dopamine) and molecular pathways that either stimulate an aversive or positive instinctual response (7) (8).

YOUR GRANDMOTHER'S GARDEN

Imagine your neighbour's children cut your grandmother's lawn and clean her windows for her each week. No charge just being neighbourly.

After a year or so of doing this, one week your grandmother brings them out a big slice of cake and glass of homemade lemonade as a reward for their hard work. The kids are overjoyed, devouring the cake and lemonade. Such a wonderful treat.

The next week, the kids are looking forward to doing the yard work in the hope of another slice of cake and work extra hard.

Your grandmother is out though and so no cake appears. The kids are disappointed.

The next week they come back and seeing that once again your grandmother is out they feel demotivated at the lack of cake and do a half-hearted job and leave.

The impact of the pleasure of the cake on their motivation has quickly waned.

In fact, it's now subconsciously an expected baseline "payment" to achieve the same standard they had been achieving previously. If your grandmother gave them cake now it is likely that she would get the original standard of work she had previously received for "free" before she gave the reward. To motivate them to work extra hard again she would need to increase the reward to something higher.

We can become accustomed to a certain level of pleasure/reward very quickly and in fact there are molecular mechanisms in the brain that affect how tolerant we are to a delay in gratification (9). Reward as an occasional motivator works well but use it too much (and alone) and you actually end up with the opposite effect you had hoped for.

This is one of the many reasons why some people on a diet find that once they have started slipping their slips become bigger and bigger until it becomes a full-on slide.

The effect of the pleasure they are receiving from the "reward" is less every time around and they need to increase the stakes to get the same pleasure reward.

Pain, however, is something quite different. Most people will go to extreme lengths to avoid pain as much as possible. As a result, I find, it is an even better motivator than pleasure.

Imagine your grandmother had instead offered to pay them £50 for their work once a month. However, she also told them for every weed she found and every patch of grass left uncut she would permanently dock them $5.

It's likely the kids would be motivated by the thought of the reward but they would probably do an extra special job each week at the thought of losing $5 permanently for every mistake. They'd probably do an outstanding job for the same money each week simply to avoid losing cash.

The perceived pain of losing something or having to do something you don't want to do is a great motivator.

We're going to use both pain and pleasure in this program to ensure you're getting the best of both effects. The Triple 'H' principle therefore hotwires your brain by using your baser instincts to ensure that you do the best you can do.

SETTING UP YOUR MONTHLY GOAL TRACKER

On the following pages you'll find the Monthly Goal Tracker form. You will use one of these for each principle. To be clear, you will have three of these on the go at any one time.

Although we are doing a three month cycle we are only going to plan one month at a time. This will allow us to adjust if things go astray or if we do even better than expected one month. (We'll come back to that in a later chapter don't worry).

Step 1:

In the previous exercise you identified your major goal for each of the 'H's - **insert that goal in the "Overall Goal" Box.**

Now for the fun bit!

Step 2:

Decide on a reward for completing your overall goal.

Make it something big enough to motivate you. Something that will improve your life by itself. Keep it realistic though. No point writing down a £300K car if you only earn minimum wage!

Step 3:

Give yourself a **consequence** for missing your overall goal target.

Yes, you read that right. *You're going to be punished for missing a goal!*

This is, in fact, a very key part. The consequence has to be something you ***really*** don't want to do.

My recommendation is giving money to a cause that you really, really, really don't agree with. It has to be enough money that you can afford it but it would be uncomfortable to lose. I've done these many times and can honestly say I've never had to give it to them.

Why? Well, usually the thought of funding something you don't agree with is enough to push you beyond your usual apathy.

If you're going down this route then before you start you **must** take the money out **in cash**, put it in an envelope, seal it, put the appropriate postage and write the address of the cause on the front. This way there will be minimal resistance to following through.

You could even give it to a loved one and explain that if you don't hit your goal they have to post it.

Some people put the exact money they would need to buy their reward in the envelope. That way they double up the power of the process. You're not only funding your nemesis but they are getting your big reward too – or so it feels.

It doesn't have to be money though. It could be a task that you really don't want to do. Something big enough that you really wouldn't do it unless you've been forced to.

It mustn't put you (or anyone else) in any danger or damage your health though, let's be clear about that.

These overall rewards and consequences will follow through for the 3 months that we're doing the program so you've just saved yourself a bit of work later – well done!

Step 4:

Break down your overall goal into 3 **equal** chunks and enter your first monthly goal onto the sheet.

Maybe the chunks won't be equal. That's ok, this is your journey. Just break it down so that you're not trying to tackle it all at once.

If you're starting something brand new or trying to start a new daily habit I recommend ramping up the levels over the course of the months to ensure that you're not setting yourself up for an immediate miss. Make sure your monthly goal accommodates for that.

You can also enter some examples of the types of activities that you can use to achieve that goal.

Step 5:

Decide on some rewards and consequences for this month's goal and enter them into the sheet.

Try and make these rewards and consequences related to the goal you're trying to achieve. Something that will help you achieve even better next month.

For example, if your goal is to get 10K run ready in three months then you might reward yourself with a new set of running shoes in month one. Your consequence might be to do 100 squats a day for the first week of next month.

The new shoes will improve your performance and likely re-motivate you for a couple of weeks. The thought of extra leg work however on top of your training likely will put you off missing the target too. If you did have to do the consequence the extra squats are likely to increase your leg strength and actually help you do even better in month 2 as well. Win:Win!

One of the places I see people fall off the wagon and miss their goals is that sometimes they aren't quite sure what they should be doing to keep moving forward. This is where the Triple H Principles gets detailed to maximise your chances of success.

Step 6:

Break down this month's goal into weekly bites.

Even a month's goal can be somewhat hard to get your teeth into.

What do you need to do each week to ensure that you can't miss your monthly goal? Break it down into weekly mini-goals.

We aren't going to go as far as a daily goal (unless you want to) but there is space on the form for you to check off (or not) your progress through the week for your goal.

Step 7:

You've guessed it! Enter some rewards and consequences for each week's goal.

These rewards again should try and be tied to the overall goal and help you on your way but be much smaller than the monthly ones. What little thing could you look forward to? What smaller thing could your consequence be?

For example, if you're aiming to live more in the present then you might have set yourself a task to meditate or have mindful moments a certain number of times a week.

Personally, I use coloring in as a method of achieving this and so I might reward myself with some new pencils if I achieve week one. I might make myself do the dishes by hand though for the next week if I miss. Why? Because if I'm doing the dishes I can use that menial task time to focus on breathing and take it as a mindful moment - increasing my chances of success the following week.

If you're doing something physical maybe one week you can treat yourself to some nice relaxing bath salts for those aching muscles and the next week have the reward to be able to use them. It's all about thinking about those little things that will keep you moving forward.

The last step is an easy one don't worry:

Step 8:

Place your monthly goal trackers somewhere you'll see them several times a day (e.g. on the fridge).

These sheets are going to help you stay on track. They're going to remind you what you're going to gain that week if you succeed and what you're going to have to do if you skip that gym session. Hiding them in a drawer is therefore counter productive.

There is also space on the sheet for you to check off each day as you complete it or plan in what you're going to do each day if you prefer.

So we're all set! You've gone from not really knowing what you need to do to maximize your satisfaction to knowing what you need to do each day to improve it in just 3 months.

Even more importantly you've got the rewards and consequences planned out that will help you stay on track.

It's time to get started.

No more waiting around.

Right now.

I mean it!

What can you do right this very moment to get you started?

Go do it now!

I'll wait…

Done? AWESOME! You're now one step closer than you were 5 minutes ago! Great job!

Monthly Goal Tracker

H_______ Goal		Overall Completion Reward		Overall Miss Consequence	
		Month Completion Reward		Month Miss Consequence	
Activities					

		M	T	W	T	F	S	S		Completion Reward	Miss Consequence
Week 1 Goal											
Week 2 Goal											
Week 3 Goal											
Week 4 Goal											

RECRUITING YOUR CHEERLEADERS

IN THIS SECTION YOU WILL LEARN

- THE IMPORTANCE OF GOOD SUPPORT
- HOW TO CHOOSE THE RIGHT LIFE COACH FOR YOU
- THE PROS AND CONS OF ONLINE SUPPORT GROUPS
- A WARNING ABOUT LOVED ONES

I have a mentor. I have... guides. I have a lot of guides. Not a lot, but people whose opinions I really respect and who I will turn to.

Jake Gyllenhaal

All that hard work of putting together the plans, rewards, consequences is something that should be celebrated, well done!

Firstly, you have not only proved to yourself how much you actually **want** to change and work on these things by persisting through the exercises (if you weren't serious you'd have given up pretty fast).

Secondly, you've now got a plan in place that rewards you for progress and gives you strong consequences for not following through. You're primed for success!

Now is the time to get started on the journey itself. Planning is all well and good but it must be followed up with real actions to be successful. There is one further action you can take to further increase your chances of success though that I highly recommend – find a cheerleader.

Not necessarily one with pom-poms but the concept is the same. Someone who is going to give you a positive cheer and push when things get tough. Someone who will also call you out when you're making excuses and help you see the positive vision you've set out. You'll need to share with them all your plans and help them understand your vision so that they know where you are coming from and what they're cheering for.

How do you select this person though? Sharing these deeply personal things can be tricky as often we worry enough about what the people we care about think of us without adding to the mix. There are three schools of thought on this:

HIRE A QUALIFIED INDEPENDENT LIFE COACH

Yes, of course, as a Life Coach myself I would say that right? Of course, I see the benefits of coaching myself both on the people I work with but also as someone who has had many different coaches myself over the years and seen the benefits.

The advantage of an independent coach is just that, they're independent. You've hired them specifically to help you succeed. It's their job. They've no personal interests in your journey going any way but successfully. They are also skilled with the appropriate tools, phrases and approaches to fit when both your successful and challenging segments to keep you moving in the right direction.

How do I select the right coach for me? There are hundreds and hundreds of people out there claiming to be coaches these days.

1. *Make sure they have a qualification.*

Whilst life experience is all well and good, you can't prove it very easily. At least if someone has a qualification you know they've had to undergo some sort of testing and prove they know what they're talking about.

2. Look for accreditation by a professional body.

Professional bodies will only allow members who have agreed to be held to certain standards as well as proved a certain level of experience and qualification to use the term “accredited”. You’re putting your success in their hands – make sure they’re accountable to someone should things go wrong!

3. Look for publications and free resources

These could be scientific papers in the field or relevant books they’ve written; videos, blogs, event appearances, etc. This ensures that they have enough knowledge to apply to a broad number of situations that will therefore potentially be applicable to anything you could hit along the way.

Free resources also ensure that they aren't just trying to pump as much money out of you as possible – they genuinely care about helping people.

Most importantly though it gives you a chance to get a feel for their style and thoughts. For a coaching relationship to work you need to be comfortable with each other. If you're not looking for a drill sergeant then those people that angry talk in their videos might not be for you!

Most importantly make sure that you "click"

Any reputable coach will offer an introductory session for free.

This is actually as much for the coach as you. We're all human beings and so not everyone "clicks" with everyone. If a coach doesn't click with a client it doesn't make for a strong partnership and will likely pass you on to someone else who is more likely to fit with your needs.

Make sure that you speak up if you don't feel they are for you and move on – don't let them flatter you into a partnership that isn't going to work for you.

LOOK FOR A FREE ONLINE MENTOR OR SUPPORT GROUP

There's lots of support groups on social media for everything you can dream of.

Pro: This is a fantastic source of free support and advice from many different everyday people who have been/are going through what you're about to start doing.

Con: You have no idea who these people are, whether they are lying or not and whether they have any qualifications at all to help you. You also open yourself up to trolls and con artists targeting people vulnerable to the topics that you're looking to work on.

FIND A PERSON YOU KNOW AND TRUST AND BITE THE BULLET

To me this is the hardest one but it works for many.

Sometimes it's your partner or parent. Others use a best friend.

This must be someone you're comfortable sharing your plans with and are confident that they are going to support you,

You also need to think carefully here about whether they could have an agenda of their own, conscious or unconscious. Could they have a reason to try and steer your journey in a particular direction?

For example, if you're trying to lose weight – will your overweight partner resent the weight you lose and so (inadvertently) not always give you the encouragement you need? Maybe in the subconscious hope that you don't succeed so that they don't feel guilt for not doing it too? I'm not claiming these things are done on purpose, but human beings are driven by many subconscious impulses every day that we aren't even aware of. *Proceed with caution on this one is my advice.*

Whichever method you use to choose a cheerleader, just having one on board can be a big boost for ensuring your success. Just having someone there to push you when you need it, be a shoulder to cry on when things are tough and to celebrate those victories makes things more fun.

A goal shared is a goal halved I always say!

WIGGLE WEEK

IN THIS SECTION YOU WILL LEARN

- **LEARN WHAT TO DO WHEN LIFE GETS IN THE WAY**

Life is not a struggle. It's a wiggle.

Peter McWilliams

OK so you've planned to within an inch of your life, you've got the world's best cheerleader waving pom-poms and doing cartwheels for your every breath – it's time to get on with moving ahead. With all the planning you've done there is absolutely no doubt what you need to do. No excuses – get on with it.

I do have to remind you though of one small thing. You suffer from a fatal disease called humanity. We all are subjects of emotions and circumstances beyond our control – both positive and negative.

In my experience, what happens in this journey is that you enter it with great excitement and ambition. You've got the vision of what you're looking to achieve and a firm plan of how to get there and you're raring to go. Nothing can stop you. You WILL go to the gym 15 times a week and survive on chicken and broccoli only. It all seems so easy when you're pumped up and planning.

Usually about day three or four though the novelty wears off and you realise that you don't like broccoli much at all (no matter how you cook it) and your boss might like you to go to work occasionally.

This is where we introduce the most important part of your journey: WIGGLE WEEK.

In the first week of the month (and **only** the first week of the month) you are free to update your weekly goals and activities for that month as required to meet the realities of life.

However, you must not change your monthly or overall goal and your weekly goals must still put you on track for success. No downgrading now. You set those goals for a reason, you ensured they were realistic and reasonable at the time (right?) – no chickening out when things get tough.

Nevertheless, maybe you were a tad ambitious to say you'd run 5 miles a day when you've never run before. In that situation I'd recommend you ramp it up gradually across the week and in fact entire month. (For an example see my pre and post wiggle week sheets in the "my story" section.)

Wiggle week is there to help you succeed not limit your success. Sometimes we are forced to take a step back to move forward.

To be clear – you can do this week once only and only in the first week of the month.

Take the opportunity to look at what you're planning and after trying it out for a week look at your success so far. Is it sustainable? Will small tweaks make a big difference? Anything you need to rethink?

With your wiggled (or not) plan in place you're all set for a month. This is the elegance of putting all the work into the planning. There is no week or even day where you're not clear what it is you need to do to keep moving forward and what you stand to gain/lose as a result.

Go chase those dreams!

MONTH 2 & BEYOND

IN THIS SECTION YOU WILL LEARN

- HOW TO PLAN YOUR SECOND MONTH OF YOUR JOURNEY
- WHAT TO DO IF THINGS AREN'T GOING TO PLAN
- HOW TO MAKE PLANNING THOSE REWARDS & CONSEQUENCES EASIER THIS MONTH

Life is a journey. When we stop, things don't go right.

Pope Francis

So, month one is coming to an end.

Are you reaping the rewards of achieving all those mini goals and even looking forward to getting your hands on your first big month goal?

Even if you're looking at a month one miss don't worry – there's still plenty of time to get back on track and potentially still hit your overall goal.

That's the elegance of this system. Every action has a potential reward and consequence so even if you're a little off track you've still got lots to gain by continuing in the right direction.

Think that your overall goal is now out of reach? That's ok too. It sucks that you're potentially going to have to take the big miss consequence at the end of the program but there's still loads of rewards and progress to look forward to. Don't give up now and lose out on all those rewards for the sake of one miss – after all who knows you might end up hitting it in the end. Just because you're going to have to take one consequence doesn't mean you have to submit yourself to them all. You have 3 goals at play remember and multiple consequences ahead.

> Just because you have one flat tyre doesn't mean you have to go slash the other three!

Keep in mind here the rewards and consequences are also not really the point – think of the improvement your life will receive for just a single percentage improvement in your scores. The rewards are there to keep you motivated but you should already be starting to feel some change in your overall satisfaction.

With a few days left of your first month take the time to review your results, celebrate your victories and examine your misses for how you can avoid them next month. With those insights under your belt we can now start planning month two.

Many people ask me,

“Why don’t you plan all three months up front ?”

...Simple....because life happens and we're human.

No one is expecting perfection from you here. Your circumstances can change as well, which might mean you need to plan month two slightly differently from month one. The process however is exactly the same.

Grab yourself some fresh month goal tracker sheets and work up those monthly and weekly goals, actions, rewards and consequences just as you did in week one. Most people find this much faster in month two than month one and a lot less daunting.

A BIG TIP TO MAKE PLANNING EASIER BEYOND MONTH 1

One big tip from my own personal experience is that in month one I struggle to think of suitable rewards and consequences.

While I'm working the program though I often think of things that would help. I put them in a list so that when further months come around I have them on hand and can do my plan even more quickly.

I personally use Evernote and amazon wish lists but asset of post-it notes, blank notebook, whiteboard, whatever (!) would work just the same.

What about month three I hear you ask...you've guessed it. Repeat. Bear in mind though this is your last month so might be a good time for an extra push to hit your goals or pull yourself back on track.

REVIEW, REFLECT & RE-CYCLE

IN THIS SECTION YOU WILL LEARN

- WHAT TO DO AFTER THE 3 MONTHS ARE UP
- WHEN TO TAKE A BREAK

Laziness is nothing more than the habit of resting before you get tired.

Jules Renard

Is that it? Month three done and dusted?

Am I suddenly super satisfied and successful?

Firstly -CONGRATULATIONS!

Even if you didn't hit your main goal just sticking to a program and slightly changing your habits for three months is a massive achievement and something you should be proud of.

I am proud of you – all of you.

Proud that you tried and continue to try. Proud that you accepted your misses and celebrated your achievements. Proud that you decided to take control of how you feel about your life.

What now? Well, that's of course up to you.

To help you decide what to do/not to do next I suggest you go back and redo the satisfaction calculations and see how your scores have changed.

Have the scores improved in line with the new satisfaction increase you're feeling in your life?

Are the low scoring areas improving?

Have your priorities changed?

Looking at your new scores are there now other things that need urgent attention?

Do you now need to swap some topics out for new ones that are now in your top 5 whilst others have dropped out?

Life is a journey and ultimately you could continue to repeat the cycle of the program to try and maximise all the scores as best you can to eternity. This is that I personally try to do. I want to be open here and give you a nudge to be realistic too.

The scores are very unlikely to **ever** be all at their maximum at the same time!

Your life priorities and situations change. You're not likely to be prioritising career progression after retirement for example and you'll have to start working on new things that you previously hadn't spent any Life Coins on – i.e. high deficit to fill!

The aim of the process is to help you focus on those areas that you need to have at their maximum for that time of your life so that you enjoy it the most in that moment.

So, as you come to the end of your first cycle ask yourself if you need and are ready for another cycle to keep things moving in a positive direction. Do you maybe need a break?

WHEN & WHY TO TAKE A BREAK

Ideally, I would take a week or two minimum in between cycles. Why? Often I push myself hard in the last month and need a rest. However sometimes I also get too close to the goals I'm working on to be able to redo the assessment objectively. In reality, I'm often too excited about the next exciting challenge that I go straight on.

This is where your cheerleader should come in again. Make the effort to have a conversation with them about the past 3 months. Review it in depth. What worked and what didn't. Get their perspective on whether you're ready for another cycle or whether you need a break.

If you decided not to take on a cheerleader then you could always write it out. I recommend writing advice to yourself in letter format and changing your name on it. Somehow writing a letter to someone with a different name makes it easier to give objective self advice. Then put it away and come back to it twenty four hours later. Re-read it and try and listen to the advice you're giving that person.

A break doesn't mean dropping all the good habits you've made over the past few months though. It's about fitting them in and making them now part of your normal routine.

After 3 months it usually makes me feel a bit weird not to be doing them anyway. It's in that way that when you are ready for your next cycle you'll be building on top of the great work you've already done and pushing your scores even higher.

Some people are very clear what they need to do next. Maybe it's just the first part of a bigger goal like a marathon training program. That's awesome. If you're ready to rock on – GO FOR IT!

Whatever your decision I hope the program has helped you feel even a fraction more satisfied with your life and given you a framework you can build on for future success.

Thank you for taking this journey with me. I wish you all the love, luck and happiness in the world.

THE TRIPLE H PRINCIPLES (SUMMARY)

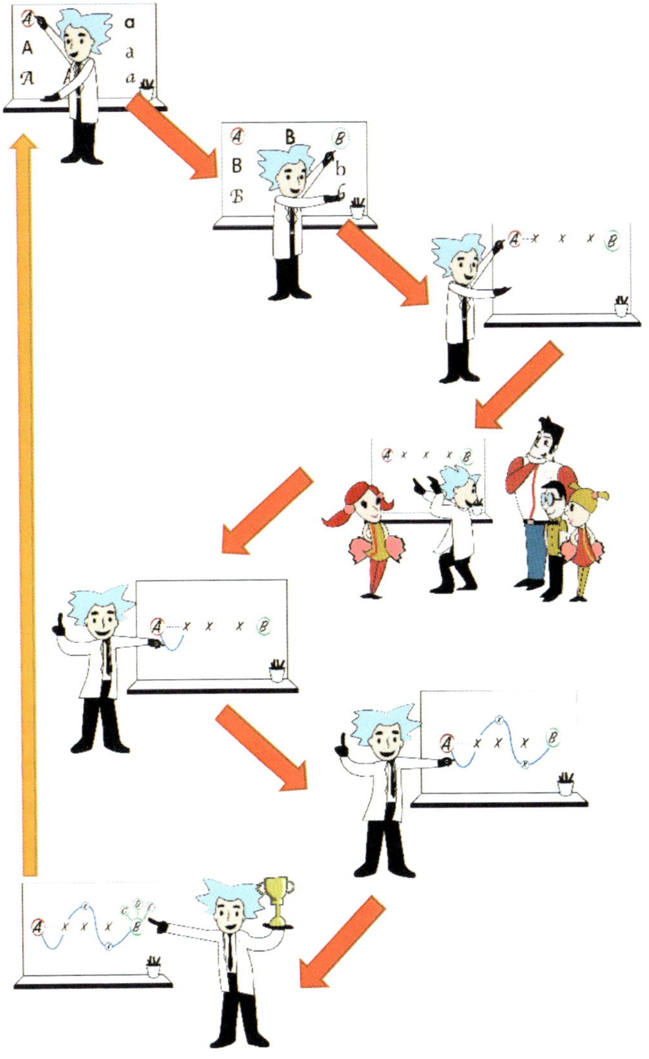

APPLYING THE METHOD IN REAL LIFE: MY MONTH 1 STORY

As I started my journey I was in recovery from a mental health crisis due to my newly diagnosed PTSD. It was triggered by various life stresses and strains that put me into an anxiety and depression downward spiral. I (as usual) had pushed myself too hard and not taken the time to step back properly before pushing on to the next exciting challenge. To put it simply I was not at my best.

(If you want to learn more about that part of my journey you can read more in my autobiography "Reliving the Past to Release the Present" available on Kindle and Amazon).

Months of comfort eating had left my six-pack well hidden under a layer of fat. I was 18 kg overweight, none of my clothes fit and I spent my days hiding from the mirror for fear of the disgust, disappointment and guilt that looking in them gave me.

This was putting further strain on my marriage due to my lack of self-confidence and lack of feeling attractive.

My mental health was now fully managed, I felt stronger than I had in a long time. I was ready to improve my situation, ready to get back to my full potential.

Due to my crisis I had had to temporarily shut down Triple H Coaching as I was in no place to be supporting and coaching others. I was facing rebuilding from the ground up. I gut wrenching and scary prospect. It all left me feeling like I was failing at my life goal to "leave the world a better place than when I entered it".

In short, I was certainly not where I want to be in life and certainly was not feeling satisfied.

It was time for a cycle of Triple H Principles. I'd been checking myself by this method one way or another for the past 20 years.

Whether it be just a few notes every day on my diary how I'm doing against each 'H' and a plan to improve things or a full formal cycle as described above. I asked myself what I would do with a coaching client who came to me in this situation. The answer was obvious. If they now felt strong enough to move ahead, I'd do a situation assessment and find out where they are, so we can plan how to improve things and boost their recovery even further.

The truth is I found this exercise tough. I procrastinated. Found 101 reasons not to do it. Not just because I thought it was time consuming but because I was somewhat scared of what I would find.

The sense of reviewing and gaining a better understanding of why I felt the way I did had certainly helped me in therapy and was helping my mental health recovery so, hard as it was, I knew I needed to do this. I needed to take my own advice for a change. After all I don't believe in getting others to do anything that I wouldn't do myself.

I'd also been itching to finish my coaching book but felt it needed something more human. Less dry. Documenting at least some of this cycle might just be what was needed. Win Win.

Working through the process and documenting it would also help me with any future coaching clients by giving a real example of the process too they can use as inspiration. Lots of pros, not many cons.

IS THAT WHERE I AM?

Once I'd run out of things to procrastinate and avoid the exercise with I took myself to a quiet spot and started to work through it.

I must admit that the exercise took less time than I had remembered it taking previously. Once I got into the swing of it again it was relatively painless.

I had a few debates about what topics to use and what the priorities were first of all. Once I'd settled on those and scored them (not a fan for maths) I bashed it into the excel sheet and alakazam the maths was all done for me.

Over the next few days I revisited it, revised scores and priorities until it felt accurate. Until in my gut I could look at it and say "Yup that feels about right."

OK, maybe that's not quite what my gut said. Maybe something more like, "Yeah that looks like the long and tall of it, sigh."

Looking at the sheet, my first feelings were fear and disappointment.

Fear - I've got a spreadsheet full of rows and numbers. What on earth do I do with all this? How do I even start understanding it let alone changing it?

Disappointment – at 34 years old I've spent my life trying to improve myself and this is all it has come to? How disappointing!

There it was in black and white. Healthy 43%, Happy 38%, Harmonious 63%. That gave me an overall satisfaction score of 48%. 48%?! 48%?!

Wow, no wonder I wasn't exactly jumping out of bed with the joys of life. I wasn't even half satisfied with my life at the moment. Certainly, room for improvement there.

As I started to review and examine each section, figures and balance between them I could finally see where I was going wrong. Why I'd felt like no matter how hard I tried it was never filling that hole inside me.

Most of my top priorities had huge life coin deficits.

It seemed as well that I'd become so focused on my big picture stuff (harmonious), my drive to leave a legacy, help others and the environment that I am in that I had left little focus on the fundamentals of Healthy and Happy. In short I was putting the horse before the cart. I was focusing on everything apart from me. With all I had been through in the past year mentally and physically it was completely the wrong balance for me at that time.

It was definitely time to take action but what to work on that will have the best overall return? I knew if I wasn't seeing benefit from my efforts pretty fast it wouldn't be good for my mental health so I needed to ensure I was choosing just the right topics.

Deep breath. OK I need to make a change. I need to improve things so that I am enjoying my life much more. In reality, the score itself doesn't matter – it's how I feel about life that is important. This is just a method of working out what needs improvement. It's not a personal judgement. It's not a report card. It's a snapshot. It's just a moment in time. I have the power to improve this and therefore feel better overall.

Overall Satisfaction Score	48%

Healthy	Overall section score 43%			
	Current Satisfaction (1-10)	Priority (1-5)	Life Coins Spent	Life Coin Deficit
Personal Development	4	5	20	30
Emotional & Mental Health	4	4	16	24
Nutrition	4	3	12	18
Sleep Quality	6	2	12	8
Relationships (Sex)	4	1	4	6

Happy	Overall section score 38%			
	Current Satisfaction (1-10)	Priority (1-5)	Life Coins Spent	Life Coin Deficit
Appearance	2	5	10	40
Ambitions & Achievements	5	4	20	20
Stress Levels	5	3	15	15
Career Satisfaction	2	2	4	16
Career Progress	8	1	8	2

Harmonious	Overall section score 63%			
	Current Satisfaction (1-10)	Priority (1-5)	Life Coins Spent	Life Coin Deficit
Legacy	7	5	35	15
Self-confidence	4	4	16	24
Home life situation/environment	8	3	24	6
Helping Others	7	2	14	6
Living in the present	5	1	5	5

THE MAX BANG FOR MY BUCK METHOD IN ACTION

The next step was to work out which of these to work on to improve things maximally. I've got a big set of whiteboards and love an excuse to draw on them so utilized the maximum bang for the buck method.

Not worrying about how messy it was it only took 10 minutes or so to come to some pretty obvious conclusions.

(For the sake of your eyes and to make it a more useful example I've redrawn it in graphical format here for you. I've also simplified it a little as there were actually more lines! You get the idea though, right?)

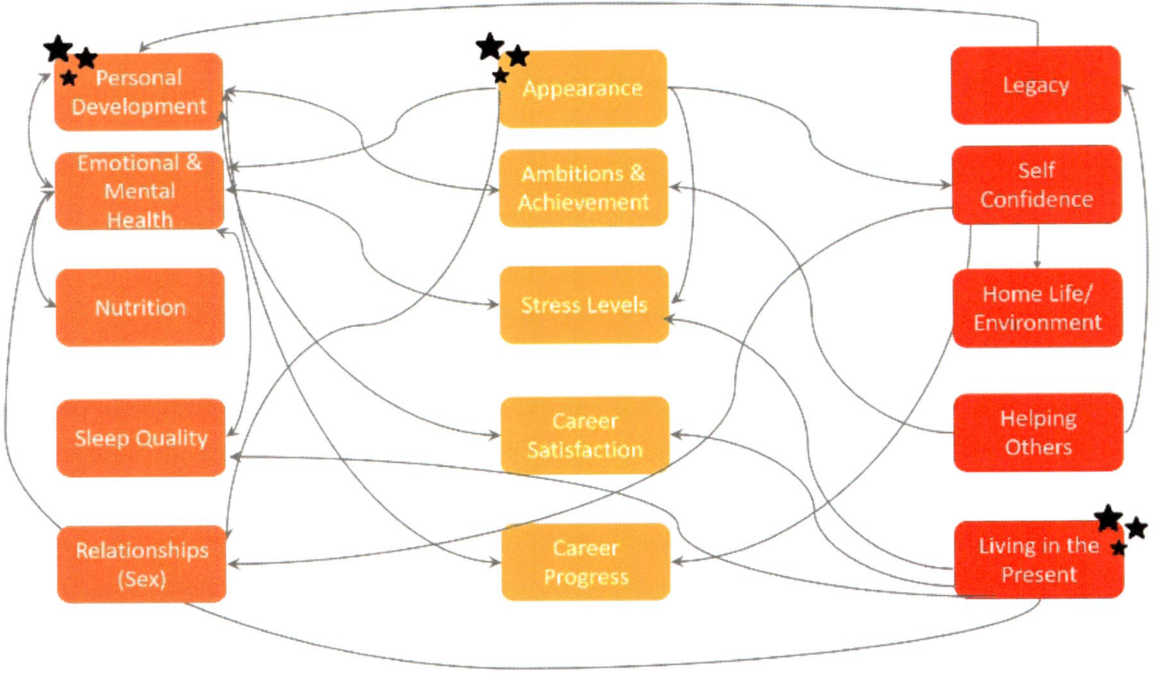

Personal Development
Emotional & Mental Health
Nutrition
Sleep Quality
Relationships (Sex)
Appearance
Ambitions & Achievement
Stress Levels
Career Satisfaction
Career Progress
Legacy
Self Confidence
Home Life/ Environment
Helping Others
Living in the Present

Everything was quite interconnected. Hard to make sense of at first. So, I started choosing them at random and seeing how much of the "map" I could cover in one step by working on that. After a while it was apparent that there were 3 areas I could work on that would affect a significant part of the board in some way: Appearance, Personal Development & Living in the Present.

It was kind of a relief.

Appearance certainly scored low and was my top hit on Happy priority. Making some serious changes there will help multiple other areas of my life and if nothing else help me live long enough to enjoy my new-found satisfaction.

I knew what I had to do. I'd been here many times and last time I'd succeeded. I'd gained the body of my dreams. I knew how to get back there. I just had to commit and execute. It was no small feat though. I had about 15 kg to lose. This was going to have to be my big goal. The other two whilst having a positive impact couldn't be too much of a burden or my mental health would suffer and I'd fail at all of them.

Living in the present was something that would benefit my life in a huge way as well as helping me preserve my mental health.

I'd tried before to do something every day to maintain a mindful state of mind but had always become distracted. Contrary to popular opinion there's no set amount of time to get a habit locked in (10). It's a process. By making it one of my three goals with the surrounding Triple H framework I hoped it would give me what I needed to get this under my belt and as a regular habit.

Mindfulness takes many forms and I jotted down a few ways I could achieve this and why it would make a big difference.

Finally, Personal Development. It's such a large topic and so many different ways to achieve it. With the large appearance goal I'd set taking priority this couldn't get out of control.

Reading is a quick way to learn and improve. I've always read slowly though and so books often take ages or go unfinished when I get distracted by something else (yes, I'm *that* person). So, maybe this was the way to push myself a little. A book a month. That was doable. I read most nights anyway and so just working out how much to read each night to achieve it would be simple.

After completing my Why form I was buzzing. I knew what I was aiming for and the fantastic improvements to my life it was all going to make.

Time to get down to planning out month one and all those awesome rewards I could earn along the way!

WHY & WHAT?

1. *Why will improving this improve my life satisfaction?*

HEALTHY

Working on developing and improving myself will boost my mental health, self-esteem, self-confidence. help me achieve better career satisfaction and find new methods of improving my day to day life.

HAPPY

To improve my appearance, I need to work on several factors that underlie it such as nutrition and fitness at the same time as looking at my outward appearance. This will cascade onto multiple areas including self-confidence.

HARMONIOUS

Much of my guilt, worry and stress comes from anticipating things that are coming in the future. Living more in the present will allow me to better appreciate the small pleasures of day to day life, reduce my stress, improve my relationships, sleep quality, work-life balance and mental health as a result.

2. *What would life with a 10/10 score for this attribute look like?*

HEALTHY

I am focused on learning and reading new methods of thinking and integrating them into my day to day life. I also pass these on to my friends, family and clients to help them improve their lives. I feel like I'm growing and improving myself little by little every day.

HAPPY

I would have a six pack again, strong defined pecks, shoulders and arms. I'd have a style of hair cut makes me feel good. I'd dress in ways that express my personality and current mood rather than to fit in or hide. I'd have a good posture, walk with my head held high and with a confident style. I'd smile and exude confidence. I'd look in the mirror and be proud of what I see. I wouldn't hesitate to wear clothes that make me feel good and are revealing. I'd be comfortable with my top off. I'd feel attractive and sexy.

HARMONIOUS

I would not spend time worrying about things outside of my control. I would appreciate every moment and be able to steer my way through the bad times with calm control whilst savouring the good moments.

PUTTING THE SOME SMART GOALS IN PLACE

HEALTHY: IN THE NEXT 3 MONTHS I AM:

...going to increase my knowledge and broaden my perspectives by reading and listening to various experts. I will be keeping notes and summaries as well as drafting appropriate exercises from 3 books.

HAPPY: IN THE NEXT 3 MONTHS I AM:

...going to regain my visible abs, increase my visible muscle mass and get back into my size 30 jeans comfortably.

HARMONIOUS: IN THE NEXT 3 MONTHS I AM:

...going to bring my mind into more regular focus for at least 10 minutes a day.

REWARDS & CONSEQUENCES

This next part took me an hour.

First of all, what was my major goal achievement reward? What was the big thing I was shooting for?

I really wanted the reward to be something that helped me stay on track after the 3 months and improved my life even more. Think Leo, think!

I started thinking about what was about to come. I work out in our garage. We call it "the gym" but it's a garage. It's grey, cold, cluttered and full of junk. Just about enough space to squeeze in and do my thing but it's not a very nice place to be.

When I had my mental health crisis I stopped working out all together and it had become even more cluttered and dirty. If I was to start working out again next week I needed to clean it out. I grabbed the hoover, cloth and a bucket of soapy water and used the time to think about what I could use as my long-term motivator.

Half way through it hit me! I'd always wanted to do this dismal "gym" up a bit and make it a more pleasant place to be but never gotten around to it. Maybe this was the time to make it better?

I could use the redecoration as my reward. Earning different parts for different goals. If I split it right I would have some amazing motivation. After all, what use is putting up mirrors if I can't repaint the walls? How much better would it be to put down proper gym flooring than just concrete? Missing any one of these would make the other too less satisfying...bingo I had my reward!

My consequence was easy- I have always used the same one and never had to pay the money. A group that I really do not agree with and couldn't stand to support.

BREAKING DOWN MONTH 1 INTO SMALLER CHUNKS

Alright major rewards and consequences done. Let's break it down!

Writing the first month and weekly goals alongside what to do each week was simple, it was the rewards and consequences that took time.

Consequences for my Happy goal were relatively simple – add some exercises or make up losses to the following week. This helps me continue to improve whilst being something that I wouldn't necessarily choose to do. Rewards came slowly but surely. Things that would help me relax, new equipment, etc.

Personal development consequences were almost impossible. How on earth do you do something that makes you develop positively that you're not keen to do? I decided to opt for things that would give me time to think or listen to pod casts but that I'd been putting off. Garden chores for example.

Living in the present was straight forward. Quick google of mindfulness gifts and then consequences that helped me live more in the present but that I definitely did not want to do unless I had to.

Everything written up all I needed to do was decide what was going to be day one.

It was the 30th of December, the answer was blindingly obvious.

Cliché as it was I set my mind on January 1st, taped the goal trackers to my fridge and smiled – "*Let's do this!*" I whispered to myself.

<table>
<tr><td>Overall Healthy Goal</td><td colspan="8">Over the next 3 months I am going to: ...increase my knowledge and broaden my perspectives by reading and listening to various experts. I will be keeping notes and summaries as well as drafting appropriate exercises from 3 books.</td><td>Overall Completion Reward</td><td>Paint for Garage Gym conversion</td><td>Overall Miss Consequence</td><td>Donate £50 to Westborough Baptist Church</td></tr>
<tr><td>This Month's Goal</td><td colspan="8">Finish reading current book (Shaun T is for Transformation) ~~and produce 4 summary documents of useful information~~.</td><td>Month Completion Reward</td><td>Udemy Course</td><td>Month Miss Consequence</td><td>Xbox ban for 1 week</td></tr>
<tr><td>Activities</td><td colspan="12">Reading & note taking. Writing Summaries weekly.</td></tr>
<tr><td></td><td></td><td>M</td><td>T</td><td>W</td><td>T</td><td>F</td><td>S</td><td>S</td><td></td><td>Completion Reward</td><td colspan="2">Miss Consequence</td></tr>
<tr><td>Week 1 Goal</td><td>Read 32 Pages ~~+ create 1 summary~~</td><td>12</td><td></td><td>12</td><td>10</td><td></td><td></td><td></td><td></td><td>Pampering Face Mask</td><td colspan="2">Hand clean dishes 1 week</td></tr>
<tr><td>Week 2 Goal</td><td>Read 32 Pages + ~~create 1 summary~~</td><td>10</td><td></td><td>20</td><td>2</td><td></td><td></td><td></td><td></td><td>Long Hot Bubble Bath</td><td colspan="2">Sweep the front drive</td></tr>
<tr><td>Week 3 Goal</td><td>Read 32 Pages + ~~create 1 summary~~</td><td></td><td>22</td><td>20</td><td></td><td></td><td></td><td></td><td></td><td>Buy new book for next month</td><td colspan="2">Read one of books currently owned</td></tr>
<tr><td>Week 4 Goal</td><td>Read 32 Pages + ~~create 1 summary~~</td><td></td><td></td><td></td><td>22</td><td></td><td></td><td></td><td></td><td>An audio book next month is ok</td><td colspan="2">Sweep the back patio</td></tr>
</table>

Overall Happy Goal	Over the next 3 months I am going to: ...regain my visible abs, increase my visible muscle mass and get back into my size 30 jeans comfortably.	Overall Completion Reward	Mirrors for Gym Conversion	Overall Miss Consequence	Donate £50 to Westborough Baptist Church
This Month's Goal	Lose 5 kg or fit back into size 32 jeans comfortably	Month Completion Reward	New Trainers	Month Miss Consequence	100 extra push ups a day for next month
Activities	Planning macros before eating (M). Cardio (C). Weights (W). Yoga (Y).				

		M	T	W	T	F	S	S		Completion Reward	Miss Consequence
Week 1 Goal	Stick to Macros 6 days a week. 2 Cardio, 2 ~~weights and~~ ~~2~~ 1 yoga session		M & Y	M	M	M	M	M	☺	Buy Lush goodies	Make up last week's misses next week
Week 2 Goal	Stick to Macros 6 days a week. ~~2~~1 Cardio, ~~2~~ weights and 2 yoga session	M & C	M	M	M		M	M & Y	☺	New earrings	1 minute cold shower every day next week
Week 3 Goal	Stick to Macros 6 days a week. 2 Cardio, ~~2~~ 1 weights and 2 yoga sessions a week.	M&W	M&Y	M	M&C			M	☹	Toppbox 1 every 2 months sub	2 min plank every day next week
Week 4 Goal	Stick to Macros 6 days a week. 2 Cardio, 2 weights and 2 yoga sessions a week.	M&W	M&C	M&Y	M&W		M&C	M&Y	☺	1 piece of new gym equipment	Make up last week's misses next week

<table>
<tr><td>Overall Harmony Goal</td><td colspan="4">Over the next 3 months I am going to:
...Bring my mind into more regular focus for at least 10 minutes a day.</td><td colspan="2">Overall Completion Reward</td><td colspan="2">Paint for Gym Conversion</td><td colspan="2">Overall Miss Consequence</td><td>Donate £50 to Westborough Baptist Church</td></tr>
<tr><td>This Month's Goal</td><td colspan="4">To build up to having 10 minutes of mindful activity at least 5 times a week</td><td colspan="2">Month Completion Reward</td><td colspan="2">Jar of Mindfulness</td><td colspan="2">Month Miss Consequence</td><td>No TV for a week</td></tr>
<tr><td>Activities</td><td colspan="11">Headspace (H), colouring in (C), breathing exercises (B), gratitude journal (G).</td></tr>
<tr><td></td><td></td><td>M</td><td>T</td><td>W</td><td>T</td><td>F</td><td>S</td><td>S</td><td></td><td>Completion Reward</td><td>Miss Consequence</td></tr>
<tr><td>Week 1 Goal</td><td>10 mindful minutes for at least 2 days this week</td><td></td><td>H</td><td></td><td>C</td><td></td><td></td><td></td><td>☺</td><td>Cinema night</td><td>Make up last week's misses next week</td></tr>
<tr><td>Week 2 Goal</td><td>10 mindful minutes for at least 3 days this week</td><td>C</td><td></td><td>H</td><td></td><td>H</td><td></td><td></td><td>☺</td><td>Aloe Vera Plant</td><td>No Facebook for a week</td></tr>
<tr><td>Week 3 Goal</td><td>10 mindful minutes for at least 4 days this week</td><td>H</td><td>H</td><td>C</td><td></td><td></td><td>B</td><td></td><td>☺</td><td>New Xbox game + game night treats</td><td>No Instagram for a week</td></tr>
<tr><td>Week 4 Goal</td><td>10 mindful minutes for at least 5 days this week</td><td>H</td><td>H</td><td>H</td><td>H</td><td>H</td><td></td><td></td><td>☺</td><td>Power Thought Cards</td><td>No iPad for a week</td></tr>
</table>

WEEK 1 – WIGGLE WEEK

Even a goal setting veteran like me needs wiggle week. Why? Because writing about goals and what you're going to do is always easier than actually doing it!

When I write it I'm full of enthusiasm and excitement I'm in the mood to push myself. I'm human though unfortunately, I have bad days. I still have dark mental health days – especially if I push myself too hard. In fact, pushing myself too hard can put me in an unstoppable downward spiral which is something that at this point in my recovery I wanted to avoid. Wiggle week therefore was crucial.

So, week one had been a struggle I must to admit. In fact, more of a struggle than I expected.

I'd done the weight loss journey before. I'd found macros the best route for me and they'd become normal for me. Although not as pleasant as eating whatever I want as much as I want it's pretty close. Part of me secretly thought that it would all just fall back into place and it would be easy, even after a year off. Unfortunately, my timing wasn't as perfect for starting as I'd hoped.

Day one on my plan was new years day. Sounded great in theory except that meant that the traditional family dinner at my mother-in-law's house. Lovely food, drink and company was top notch as usual. It did mean however that I had spent my day off macros on day one! Not the best start.

I was hit also with a couple of really dark days during the first week. When my PTSD depression hits I feel like I'm walking through tar, like I can barely keep my eyes open and all I want to do is eat sugar and fat. Not very conducive to fitting in a smaller jean size.

So, I adjusted the plans to accommodate for the potential of having those days. I used the wiggle week rule.

Instead of the same level of exercise each week I decided to start by ramping up the levels each week instead of going full on 6 days a week from week one. This meant I was still able to hit that relatively easily and just focus on staying strong and sticking to my macros. I also hoped it would give me a growing sense of satisfaction of achieving more each week, spurring me on to the next week with added zeal.

I also had to cut out the idea of writing up the summaries of my reading. Great idea but I questioned whether I would ever have actually used them. I decided I could use the time to write my notes weekly summary for this book instead of summaries that would probably never see the light of day again. That would help my progress more and ensure I didn't miss anything important.

Week one therefore was a victory all round. Tough at times but I made it through and then had the joy of ordering those Lush goodies and a nice chill out with face mask.

I must admit I “spent” the cinema night reward before the end of the week. One day early. My partner and I hit the cinema on the Saturday and enjoyed every moment of it. To be fair, I’d already hit my goal though, so it wasn’t too much of a no no.

I left week one feeling like this was actually achievable. Ready for the next challenge.

WEEK 2 – SLUMP WEEK

Ever watched Biggest Loser? If so, you’ll be familiar with the concept of the week two curse/slump.

Week one you're full of enthusiasm and your body responds quickly. On a weight loss journey that usually means you drop a good amount of weight in the first week. By week two though your body has realized what's going on and rebels. Often people even gain weight in week two as a result. Your mind has also got over the novelty of what you're doing and you're a little less enthusiastic about your tasks.

This is what I was prepared for at the start of week two. Miraculously, my weight continued to come down however and I even managed to get into a pair of 32 jeans for our end of week night on the tiles.

I could, however, very much feel the enthusiasm for my other two goals slumping though. They had started to feel more like chores and less like something new and fun.

The rewards for my healthy goal kept me going. I wanted what was on offer! I was relieved that I'd had the foresight to link them like this. Putting actually getting to use a reward from one goal as a reward for another helped stop me being too focused on one thing. I'd bought my lovely new bath goodies and was determined to get to use them that week! I moved them to a very prominent position in the bathroom to keep them front and centre of my mind.

Harmony was a different story. I love plants and really felt that adding more greenery to our environment at home would help to create a space more conducive to mindfulness. It wasn't exactly thrilling though. Thinking about the consequences of no facebook for a week was a different story. Facebook is the main platform for Triple H Coaching and many people message me to tell me how much they enjoy the videos. I didn't want to let them down. Also it's such a nice time filler when you are somewhere and feel a bit socially awkward. No way I was losing that comfort blanket either.

I pushed through. I planned and I gritted my teeth at time to make sure it got done. The pleasure/pain principle was in full effect but it was interesting to see where pain was more motivating in some places than others this week.

Week two took more willpower than the previous week but I'd still achieved my ramp up goals and was on track so far for the month. One step at a time Leo.

WEEK 3 – FRUSTRATION AND FLEXIBILITY

So, my weight stopped dropping this week. It seemed the dreaded week two slump hit my body after all – just a week late.

It hit me hard to be honest. The appearance transformation was my main goal and feeling that I'd not made progress really got me down. I knew deep down that if I just kept consistently meeting my goals and pushing on that it will happen. That doesn't make it easy at the time though.

During the week I was hit with several "F### it!" feelings and the urge to just eat whatever I wanted to feel better. This was how I'd fought off the mental darkness of the PTSD crisis in the previous year and so felt easy, natural and guaranteed to lift my mood. I resisted though. Told myself to save it all for my one macro free day and truly enjoy it all then. There's only so much damage a single day can do and the satisfaction would be greater.

Several higher stress items hit me too. Workloads were ramping up, some unpleasant personal situations and dealing with internet trolls (which still get under my skin far too much) meant that I had all the excuses I needed to let my goals slip lined up nicely to justify that F### it moment.

Somehow having to face those goal sheets on the fridge every morning and through the day helped though. Just looking at the miss consequences really made me think about how badly I wanted to fall off the wagon and what I could do to ensure I met the goal and avoided them. After all who wants to do plank *every day*?

That doesn't mean I'm not human though. I need some flexibility sometimes. Instead of full macro adherence sometimes I allowed myself to just stick to my calorie intake goal instead. The results won't be as quick (maybe why I'd stalled this week) but better than if I went completely off track. What I count as "cardio" also had to flex a bit. A long walk on the beach instead of the treadmill running for example. I got through the work week because I allowed myself to be human and found ways to hit my goals without being unreasonably strict.

Then free day finally arrived. Friday night was our night in together with Netflix, wine and good food. I bought food that I'd been craving and relaxed into enjoying it, in the knowledge I was still making progress towards my goals. I overdid it somewhat though and went to bed feeling sick, wondering why I always go to such extremes.

On Saturday I awoke still feeling a bit rough. Didn't want to eat. We went out to buy DIY supplies for my partner's latest home project.

I could feel my mood slipping. All the change and pressure was pushing me to the edge. I could feel myself teetering on the edge of a downward spiral. I was losing faith in myself and my abilities. The dark voice was telling me how stupid I was, how weak, just to hide, that I was never going to achieve my goals anyway so why try.

I got home and put my pizza in the oven. I'd planned it so that I could still have a nice treat dinner and still be on track. My mood continued to drop as my blood sugar continued to drop.

I went to get my pizza out of the oven...it was stuck to the tray. I'd forgotten to oil it first.

The voice was screaming in my head at how pathetic I was…couldn't even make a pizza. My partner was on hand to give me a hug and reassure me. I wolfed down my dinner. Still feeling empty both physically and emotionally.

Then it happened.

I spotted the left-over chocolate treats from last night. I told myself I could fit them in. I knew I couldn't. I sat and stared at them for 30 minutes.

I did some mindful breathing (tick that off the list) for 10 minutes in the hope that it would distract myself and bring me back to centre. It did. I felt very centred. My mind was centred firmly on the chocolate! So, I wolfed them down and chased them with bread and more chocolate. After all I was going to have to do the consequence anyway right? Might as well enjoy the fail.

Sunday…I'd put on more weight (of course) …was still feeling bad and wondering what's the point. Beating myself up for being so weak. Not sure what to eat.

A big part of me wanted to continue comfort eating and bury my disappointment and feelings. Still thinking that another day won't make a difference to the consequence whilst still trying to keep my eye on the longer-term goal.

I was already in my 32-inch jeans…already hit my monthly goal but a long way from the 5 kg loss I'd also hoped for.

I *could* get away with another day of eating what I like. I *could* get back on track today.

I didn't know what to do though. Neither felt easy. One was certainly more attractive than the other. Do I want to go out in the snow to feed the beast or stay in and hide and try and just eat what I have and likely get back on track?

I made it to 10:30 am without making a decision. No decision was the best I could do right now. For now coffee was all I can manage to decide to have. I'd decide more later.

Before I knew it, it was mid afternoon and I'd eaten nothing. I smiled. I felt the pressure lift. By making no decision I'd actually got myself back on track since I had a whole day's worth of food I could eat at dinner time. I got the best of both worlds and breathed a sigh of relief as I marked the big "M" in the box next to Sunday.

I had noticed though I've become laser focused on my major goal that I was missing the positive progress I'm making on my other goals. My cheerleader gave me a nudge. Highlighting the fact that I'd hit them both week on week without too much trouble. In fact, I was a little ahead of my reading goal and meditiation/colouring has really helped me bring mindfulness into my day to day life more often. It's all about perspective Leo.

Progress not Perfection is my lesson from this week. Hopefully next week my weight loss will kick back in and I'll be able to meet both the numeric as well as the clothes element of my month one goal.

WEEK 4 – REVIEW AND REDRAFT

Week four was another challenge (I didn't say this was easy did I?). I went into it though knowing I could do it. Putting my miss last week behind me and taking the challenge of the 2 minute plank as a bonus to push me even further ahead on my goal as well as getting me back on track. It definitely made me kick myself for letting chocolate get the better of me and turn a slip into a full on slide.

Feeling like I'd learned some important lessons about not making decisions and flexing my cardio to fit my current state of mind.

I found myself walking into the gym with less of an air of "let's get this over with" and more of a feeling of moving forward in the right direction. I craved to get back to doing more weights and less yoga or cardio. Definitely giving me plenty to think about in my next month planning. Maybe gradually phase up the weights instead of cardio and leave in the yoga?

As my weight naturally wiggled up and down the overall downward trend was there again thankfully. I'd got myself back on track and ended month one on a positive.

Ultimately, I had hit my month one goal of fitting back in those jeans regardless of the fact I missed my numeric goal by 1kg. I'm proud of that. After all a 4kg (8.8 lbs) in 4 weeks is nothing to be ashamed of and it is appearance I'm trying to improve not numbers on a scale.

My mindfulness and personal development goals also hit their mark. Not a single missed week! I'm really feeling a positive impact from these even though they're not my major goal.

The extra mindfulness quickly became part of my day to day life. I felt calmer. More able to think before reacting, well, most of the time. I felt more in control.

Shaun T's book had also been inspiring both in content and the fact that I read it so quickly. I know if I hadn't broken it down it probably would still be lingering on that bedside table. Knowing how much I needed to read made it feel manageable. I highly recommend the book by the way! He's had a fascinating life and the lessons he's learned helped me immensely. Just an injection of Shaun T energy once a day is a plus I say!

With month one's lessons behind me I'm now sitting down to choose my book for next month and plan out my rewards (and consequences).

I'm excited about moving forward, I'm proud of what I've achieved and determined to be more realistic with month two without putting my goal in jeopardy.

I'm also conscious that life happens though and maybe I'll need a few cycles to get there. Either way I can feel things getting better without even rerunning the numbers so it's worth every consequence that might be coming my way in the end.

Time to celebrate and enjoy the bigger rewards. Shopping for new trainers is on the calendar and the jar of mindfulness is in my amazon cart waiting for payday! Now to find which Udemy Course I want to do whilst planning month 2 and beyond! Rock on!

WORKS CITED

1. *Effect of a psychological skills training program on swimming performance and positive psychological development.* **Golby, Michael Sheard & Jim.** 2, s.l. : International Journal of Sport and Exercise Psychology, 2011, Vol. 4.

2. *The Effects of Mental Practice on Motor Skill Performance: Critical Evaluation and Meta-Analysis.* **Hinshaw, Karin E.** 1, s.l. : Imagination, Cognition and Personality, 1991, Vol. 11.

3. *Imaginative Reinforcement Learning: Computational Principles and Neural Mechanisms.* **Samuel J. Gershman, Jimmy Zhou and Cody Kommers.** 2017, Journal of Cognitive Neuroscience, pp. 2103-2113.

4. **Peters, Steve.** *The Chimp Paradox.* s.l. : Penguin Publishing Group, 2012.

5. *No pain no gain? Pursuing a competing goal inhibits avoidance behavior.* **Stefaan Van Damme, Dimitri M.L.Van Ryckeghem,Fran Wyffe lsLore Van Hulle, Geert Crombez.** 4, s.l. : Pain, 2012, Vol. 153.

6. *Anxiety sensitivity, fear, and avoidance behavior in headache pain.* **Peter J.Norton, Gordon J.G.Asmundson.** 1-2, s.l. : Pain, 2004, Vol. 111.

7. *Modulation for emergent networks: Serotonin and dopamine.* **Juyang Weng, Stephen Paslaski, James Daly, Courtland Van Dam, Jacob Brown.** s.l. : Neural Networks, 2013, Vol. 41.

8. *A common neurobiology for pain and pleasure.* **Tracey, Siri Leknes & Irene.** s.l. : Nature Reviews Neuroscience, 2008, Vol. 9.

9. *Serotonin and tolerance to delay of reward in rats.* **Thiébot, J.-C. BizotC. Le BihanA. J. PuechM. HamonM.-H.** 4, 1999, Vol. 146.

10. **Selk, Jason.** Habit Formation: The 21 day Myth. *Forbes.* 2013.

Thank you for purchasing the

SUPER TECHNICOLOUR EDITION

of

Life Satisfaction: A Scientist's Guide!

To find out more about exclusive offers available to you as a thank you please go to:

WWW.TRIPLEHCOACHING.COM/STE.HTML

ABOUT THE AUTHOR

Dr Leo Lafferty-Whyte grew up in the North East of Scotland in the 80's and 90's. As a young gay man in a small fishing village he suffered mental and physical abuse on a daily basis. He used his past traumas to fuel his hunger for self improvement and adopted the life goal of leaving the world a better place than when he entered it.

After several years' experience and receiving his life coaching accreditation Leo launched Triple 'H' Coaching in 2016 and the Triple H Coaching mobile app in the same year. By providing videos and exercises for free in the app Leo aimed to ensure that life coaching was available to everyone without the often high barrier of fees.

As well as this book and multiple scientific publications; Leo's first book hit the top 10 ranking in kindle LGBT true Life stories shortly after publication.

OTHER TITLES BY THE AUTHOR

RELIVING THE PAST TO RELEASE THE PRESENT. (TRAUMATIC MEMORIES AND LETTERS TO MY YOUNGER SELF).

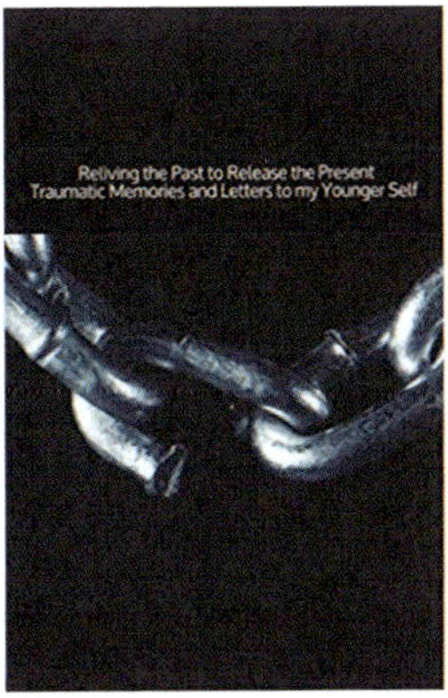

Leo seems to be a cheery successful man. He has risen to a senior management level in his career at a young age, has a happy family life and hobbies. What people don't know is the darkness that torments him every day underneath it all.

This is a chronological collection of traumatic memories from Leo's young to middle aged life in north east Scotland. At the end of each section Leo writes a letter to himself at that time with the intent of helping himself look at things differently. He also provides key reflections and lessons learned that are applicable to anyone in similar situations.

★★★★★ Outstanding!!

★★★★★ A very brave and honest book

★★★★★ Insightful and hopeful account of trauma and recovery.

★★★★★ A well-written, honest and brave account from Dr L-W ...

THANKS

There are so many people I'd like to thank for contributing to and supporting me through this book and the associated journey that to name them all would be a novel in itself. There are a couple however I would like to call out by name.

Firstly, Ross Holmes for bringing "Sci" the scientist to life and not inflicting my terrible drawing skills on the world in print.

Secondly, I owe a debt of thanks to author Laura-Jane Clements for her support and her advice on the title and theme of this book.

Of course, the largest thanks must go to my rock, my cheerleader, my partner-in-crime and grounding critic Alan. Thank you for your support through the process, fabulous cover design and patience with endless discussions.

ILLUSTRATIONS BY

RJH

GRAPHIC DESIGN

ILLUSTRATION

www.rossjholmes.com

@rossjholmes

For more information or to apply to be coached directly by Leo:

Go to **www.triplehcoaching.com**

or email **info@triplehcoaching.com**.

Join us on Facebook:

www.facebook.com/triplehcoaching

Join us on Twitter: @triplehcoaching

25429193R00123

Printed in Poland
by Amazon Fulfillment
Poland Sp. z o.o., Wrocław